CATHEDRAL

www.hmhbooks.com

The text of this book is set in Times New Roman and
Berkeley Oldstyle.
The Library of Congress Cataloging-in-Publication
data is on file.

ISBN 978-0-544-10000-8

Manufactured in China
SCP 10 9 8 7 6 5 4 3 2 1
4500427937

CATHEDRAL

HOUGHTON MIFFLIN HARCOURT BOOKS FOR YOUNG READERS
Houghton Mifflin Harcourt
Boston New York

Cathedral had been in print for more than thirty-five years and *Castle* for more than thirty when the vigilant people at HMH broached the subject of refreshing those old chestnuts. The most obvious way of breathing new life into the books was to add color to the more staid and I suppose slightly old-fashioned pen-and-ink drawings. I considered the proposal, but it felt wrong to layer color over cross-hatching, no matter how subtle the colors might be. Building up layers of line is what you do when you don't have color to work with. And in 1973, when *Cathedral* was published, black and white was the only realistic way of producing such a large book by an unknown author/illustrator. Although I declined the colorization option, the possibility of seeing those two imposing structures and their builders in full color was just too intriguing. Almost overnight, a dubious proposition became an irresistible opportunity.

A year and a half later, I was finished with both books. More than half the illustrations in *Castle* display little or no resemblance to their predecessors. All of *Cathedral's* illustrations had been reworked from scratch and everything was now in color.

In the original versions, cross sections were a useful shorthand when I had not yet worked out details I didn't quite understand. As soon as I started work, I realized just how many cross sections I had included and replaced them with more fully realized three-dimensional views. Exposure to a number of experts as we adapted the stories to television made it possible to clarify sequences of construction and improve on many smaller details in both books.

I updated the information whenever I could, but what remains consistent between these new editions and the originals is the use of perspective and dramatic points of view. It has always been my goal to draw my readers into the process, to make them feel like participants in the creation of these structures rather than merely curious but faraway bystanders.

Stories about architecture are stories about people. And these two structures remind us that when people work together in the pursuit of some grand scheme, extraordinary things are possible. That these buildings are still standing after so many centuries recalls a level of determination and commitment necessary to overcome all manner of practical problems and technological limitations. It also underscores the value of common sense—as there is little margin for error when stacking large stone blocks a hundred feet into the air.

Although motivated by quite different visions and shaped in response to unique requirements, both structures continue to impress. Castles such as those built by King Edward I in Wales were intended to crush the rebellious spirit of those whose lands they dominated as much as to resist attack. They succeeded at both, which is remarkable, considering that the buildings were completed in just five years.

The great gothic cathedrals, on the other hand, were intended to elevate the spirits of all who came to pray, learn, and worship. They remain inspirational in both their immense scale and beauty. That they are still in use is nothing short of astonishing.

Whatever magical or superhuman notions these buildings may stir, castles and cathedrals are tangible reminders of human potential. Understanding how they came to be is just the first step in recognizing that potential in each of us.

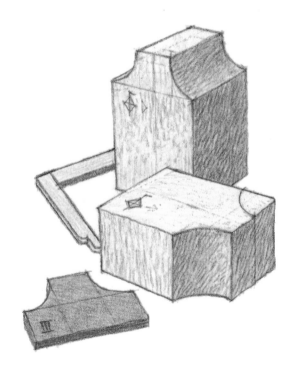

INTRODUCTION

For hundreds of years the people of Europe were taught by the church that God was the most important force in their lives. If they prospered, they thanked God for His kindness. If they suffered, they begged for God's mercy, for surely He was punishing them.

In the thirteenth century God was especially good to the people of France. The alliance of a powerful monarchy and an equally powerful clergy helped spread peace, prosperity, and learning across the land. The population grew, crops were plentiful, and business was booming. There were no wars to fight, at least on French soil, and the great plague wasn't even a twinkle in some poor flea's eye.

God's blessings were evident, and nowhere more so than in the cities. To express their gratitude and to help insure that He would continue to favor them, many of these vibrant and thriving communities undertook the building of new cathedrals of unprecedented scale and magnificence.

Although the cathedral in this story is imaginary, the methods of its construction correspond closely to the actual construction of a Gothic cathedral. While the builders too are imaginary, their single-mindedness, their spirit, and their incredible courage are typical of the people of twelfth-, thirteenth-, and fourteenth-century Europe whose towering dreams still stand today.

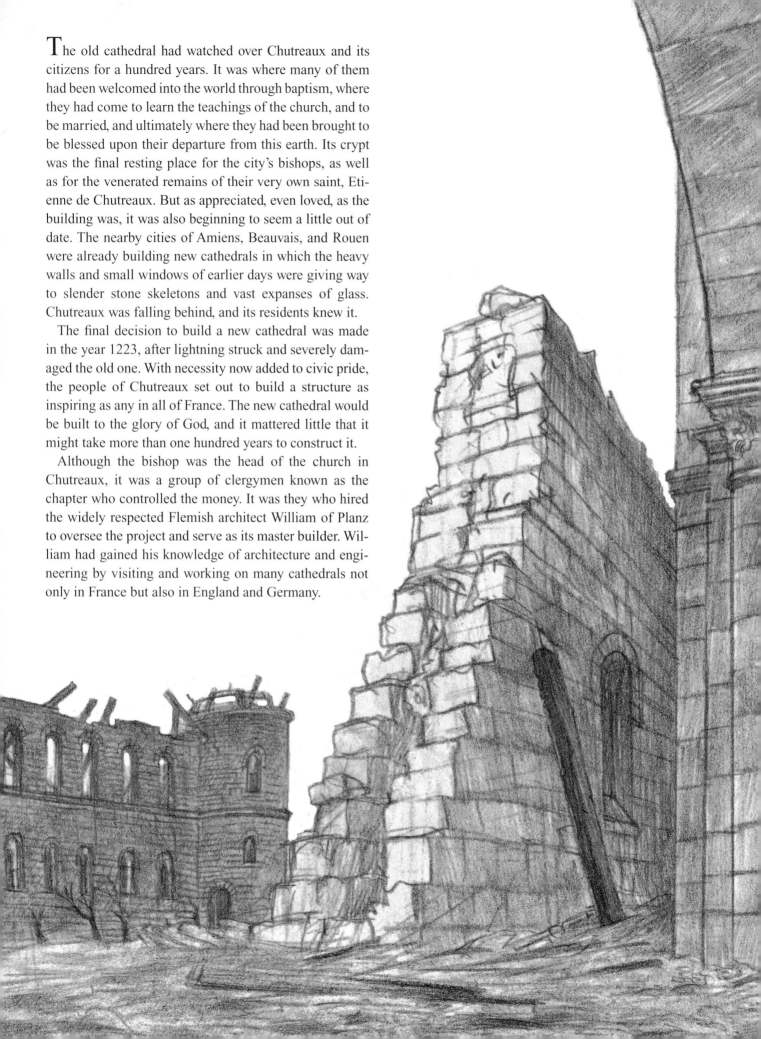

The old cathedral had watched over Chutreaux and its citizens for a hundred years. It was where many of them had been welcomed into the world through baptism, where they had come to learn the teachings of the church, and to be married, and ultimately where they had been brought to be blessed upon their departure from this earth. Its crypt was the final resting place for the city's bishops, as well as for the venerated remains of their very own saint, Etienne de Chutreaux. But as appreciated, even loved, as the building was, it was also beginning to seem a little out of date. The nearby cities of Amiens, Beauvais, and Rouen were already building new cathedrals in which the heavy walls and small windows of earlier days were giving way to slender stone skeletons and vast expanses of glass. Chutreaux was falling behind, and its residents knew it.

The final decision to build a new cathedral was made in the year 1223, after lightning struck and severely damaged the old one. With necessity now added to civic pride, the people of Chutreaux set out to build a structure as inspiring as any in all of France. The new cathedral would be built to the glory of God, and it mattered little that it might take more than one hundred years to construct it.

Although the bishop was the head of the church in Chutreaux, it was a group of clergymen known as the chapter who controlled the money. It was they who hired the widely respected Flemish architect William of Planz to oversee the project and serve as its master builder. William had gained his knowledge of architecture and engineering by visiting and working on many cathedrals not only in France but also in England and Germany.

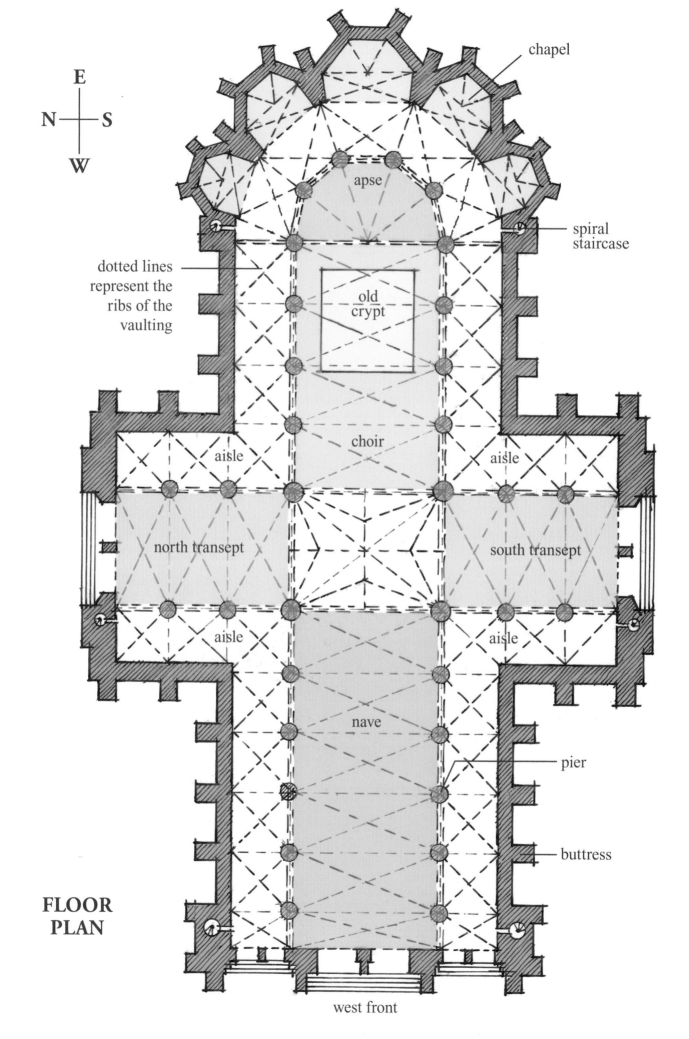

E
N — S
W

chapel

spiral staircase

dotted lines represent the ribs of the vaulting

apse

old crypt

choir

aisle

aisle

north transept

south transept

aisle

aisle

nave

pier

buttress

FLOOR PLAN

west front

After weeks of planning and sketching, William presented his final designs to the bishop and the chapter. The floor plan, which took the traditional form of a cross, was drawn on a specially prepared sheet of plaster. On a sheet of vellum, he had drawn a cross section of the building to show the main structure from the foundations all the way up to the roof and next to it an elevation of a typical section of the interior wall from floor to ceiling.

On May 24, 1224, the chapter gave its enthusiastic approval to William's design, and work began.

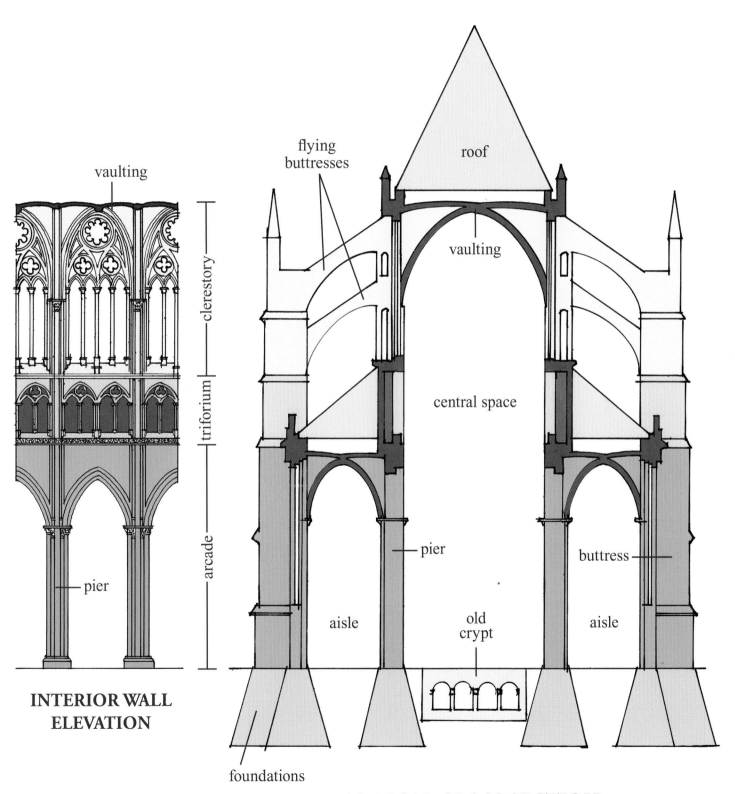

INTERIOR WALL ELEVATION

vaulting

clerestory

triforium

arcade

pier

TYPICAL CROSS SECTION

flying buttresses

roof

vaulting

central space

pier

buttress

aisle

old crypt

aisle

foundations

The first task was to gather the necessary workers and the masters who would oversee them. As was customary, William had not come to Chutreaux alone. He was accompanied by several of his most trusted craftsmen, including a master mason, carpenter, and sculptor. The rest of the master craftsmen were hired from the area, including a quarryman, a stonecutter, a mortar maker, a blacksmith, a roofer, and a glassmaker.

In addition to running their particular workshops, each master was responsible for the training of apprentices, or assistants who one day hoped to become masters themselves. Most of the heavy work was done by laborers, men with no particular skill. Some came from Chutreaux, some from the surrounding countryside.

lever

saw

mallet
and chisel

dividers

measuring
stick

pickax

mistake

square

ax

two-man
saw

saws

adze

Most of the tools used by the various craftsmen were
made of wood and iron. All the metalwork was done by
a blacksmith, and the wooden pieces were produced by
skilled woodworkers.

wood chisel

brace

auger

bit

13

By mid-June, laborers were busy clearing the site for the new cathedral. Beginning at the eastern end where the apse and choir would eventually stand, they removed all that remained of the old building except for the crypt, which, with its precious contents, would be incorporated into the new structure. As the new cathedral was to be much larger than its predecessor, a number of houses, including the bishop's palace, which had been damaged during the fire, had to be either demolished or dismantled and relocated.

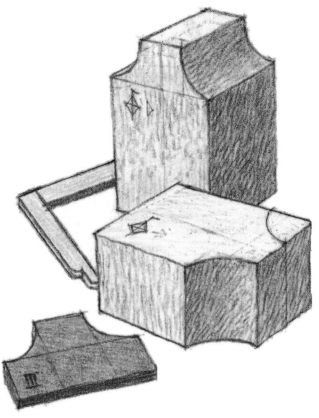

Even while William was still designing, his master quarryman had been touring a number of sites in the Somme valley, an area rich in limestone. After comparing the quality of the stone, he made arrangements on behalf of the chapter to rent an existing quarry for the duration of the project. As soon as the plans were approved, he ordered the construction of several new stonecutting sheds and a forge where the blacksmith could make and repair tools.

As blocks of stone were pried free of the quarry face, laborers delivered them to one of the workshops, where stonecutters chiseled out the rough shape following a pattern or template supplied by the master mason. Each stone was marked twice, once to show which stonecutter had actually shaped it so that he would be paid, and once to show its final location in the cathedral.

At the same time, a master carpenter and several of his apprentices, along with one hundred and fifty laborers, were busily harvesting timber in the forest of Chantilly for the construction of scaffolding, workshops, and hoisting machines.

William wanted to be sure that by the time construction began, a steady supply of building material would always be available. Most of the stone and timber arrived by boat at the city dock, where it was loaded onto waiting carts and hauled up to the site by teams of oxen. The first sacks of lime from a local kiln were also beginning to pile up under the sloping roof of the mortar makers' shed.

As soon as the east end of the site had been sufficiently cleared, William had marked out the location of the apse and choir with wooden stakes. Now teams of laborers were busily digging the holes for the foundations, which would support the building and prevent it from settling unevenly. Around the edge of the site, and a safe distance from the excavations, and the small mountains of earth they produced, carpenters built a number of workshops and sheds in which the craftsmen could eat, rest, and work in bad weather. They also built a second forge for the production of tools and nails.

The blessing of the first foundation stone on April 14, 1225, began a construction project almost as massive as that of the cathedral itself, but one that would disappear entirely below the ground.

The first layer of foundation stones was set on a bed of pebbles and clay at the bottom of the excavation. As the blocks were nudged into place, masons troweled a thin layer of mortar between them. This precise mixture of sand, lime, and water was produced by mortar men and delivered to the masons by laborers.

With his level, the master mason continually checked to make sure each course of stone was perfectly horizontal. Any carelessness in the construction of the foundations could endanger the structure that would eventually stand on top of them.

As the masons gradually worked their way around the choir, carpenters built a roof over the crypt to protect it from the rain and snow.

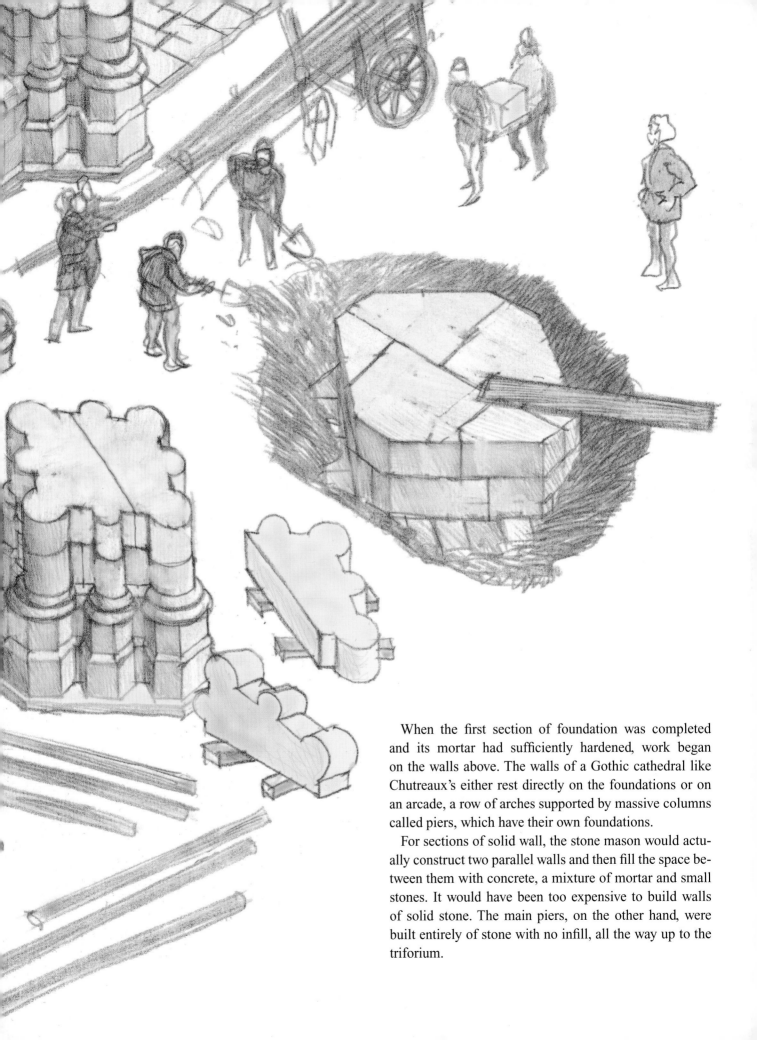

When the first section of foundation was completed and its mortar had sufficiently hardened, work began on the walls above. The walls of a Gothic cathedral like Chutreaux's either rest directly on the foundations or on an arcade, a row of arches supported by massive columns called piers, which have their own foundations.

For sections of solid wall, the stone mason would actually construct two parallel walls and then fill the space between them with concrete, a mixture of mortar and small stones. It would have been too expensive to build walls of solid stone. The main piers, on the other hand, were built entirely of stone with no infill, all the way up to the triforium.

The vertical mullions and intricate tracery that made up the framework of the windows, all of which was carefully cut from templates, were cemented into place as the walls were being built. But even before the window level was reached, wooden scaffolding had become a necessity for supporting hoists as well as movable platforms for the workers. The scaffolding was made of poles lashed to-gether with rope, and the platforms, called hurdles, were made of woven twigs.

Next to one of the chapels surrounding the apse, masons were building a spiral staircase to carry workers, tools, and even some materials up to the triforium. By the time the cathedral was finished, several such staircases would be in place, some of which reached all the way to the roof.

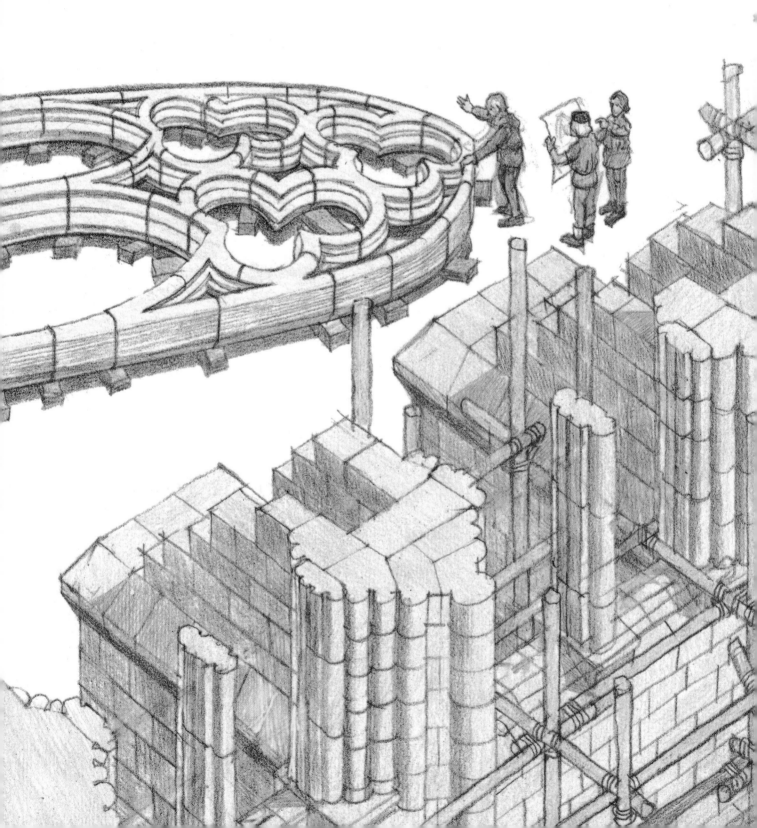

By 1235 many of the piers of the arcade were complete and work began on the arches that would link them. These were built of wedge-shaped blocks of stone called voussoirs over temporary wooden frames called centerings. Once the wall above each arch was in place and its mortar had set, the centering could be lowered and used elsewhere.

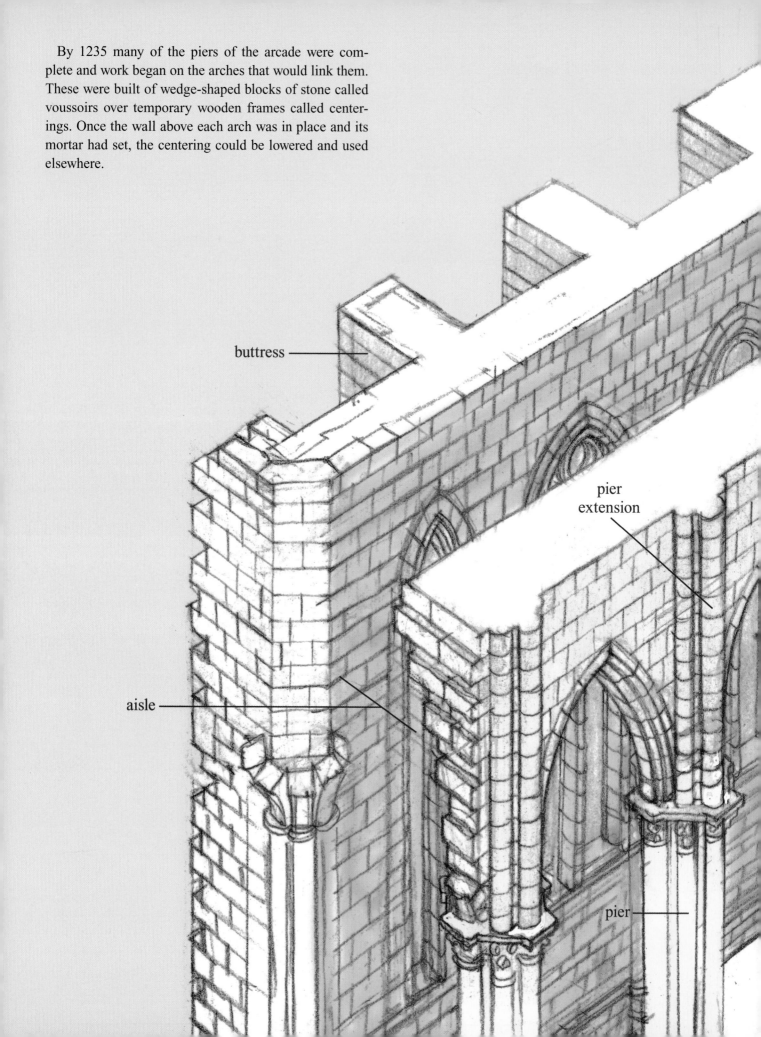

buttress

pier extension

aisle

pier

The smaller arches of the triforium as well as the narrow passageway behind them were built next on top of the arcade. As each section of the triforium was finished, it was tied to the top of the outer wall by a wooden roof. The aisle between the arcade and the outer wall was then covered by a vaulted ceiling. Once again wooden centerings were used—this time to build the arches that would help support the vaulting.

By the summer of 1242, the pier extensions and window tracery of the clerestory were visible. Given the scarcity and expense of very tall timbers, the scaffolding required for everything above the triforium was supported by the walls themselves rather than the floor.

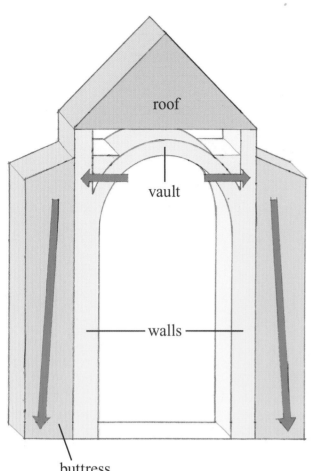

roof

vault

walls

buttress

William knew that the arch-shaped ceiling that would eventually cover his cathedral would tend to push the walls outward. In order to protect the walls, these destructive forces would need to be counteracted in some way. In earlier churches, the problem was solved by building heavy stone towers called buttresses right up against the walls and between the relatively small windows. But when aisles were needed around the central space, the buttresses were built away from the high walls. They were then connected to the high walls by stone arches called flying buttresses. The outward forces would travel across the flying buttresses and down through the buttresses to the foundations below.

When a section of wall and its adjacent buttresses reached a certain height, wooden centerings and scaffolding were installed between them. These would not only support the flying buttresses during their construction, they would also give the entire structure additional stability.

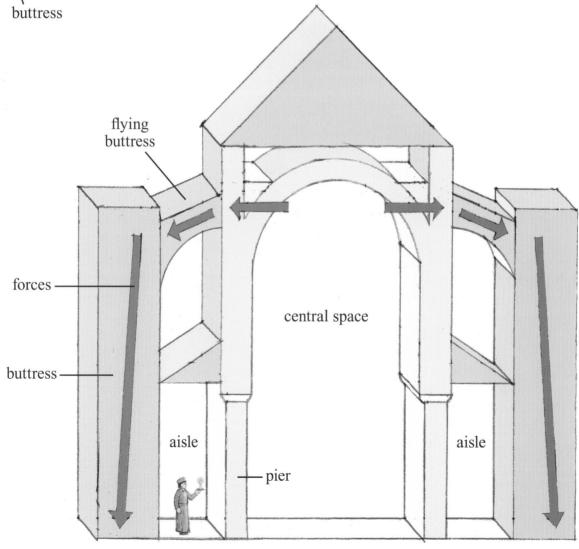

flying buttress

forces

buttress

central space

aisle

aisle

pier

Even as tracery was being installed, window makers were already at work preparing for the time when they would replace the masons on the scaffolding. Most of the windows would use a combination of clear glass—to illuminate the interior space—along with small areas of decorative stained glass. A number of special windows to be filled entirely with stained glass had also been ordered. Because of their expense, these windows were paid for by wealthy individuals or professional organizations.

Since these windows were meant to tell specific stories, the window makers and clergymen worked closely together on their design.

The glass used in all the windows was made from a combination of beechwood ash and washed sand melted together at high temperatures. To achieve the different colors, particular kinds of metals, vegetation, and even old glass were added to the mix. All the glass was produced in workshops located near surrounding forests, where plenty of wood was available for fueling the furnaces.

There were two main ways of making the glass, but both began by first scooping up a ball of molten glass on the end of a hollow pipe and blowing air into it. In one method the glass was blown up like a balloon before being transferred to a solid pipe called a punti. The blow pipe was then cut free and the sphere, now with a hole in it, was spun quickly, which forced it to open up into a flat circular shape. It was then removed from the punti and allowed to cool. The second method involved blowing up the glass while simultaneously rolling it on a hard surface to form a cylinder. When the cylinder reached the right size, the ends were cut off and it was sliced down the middle and opened to form a flat sheet.

At each window maker's shop, a full-size plan for a section of a window was first drawn on a whitewashed bench. Every piece of glass was laid over this pattern before being cut to the exact size and shape using a pointed steel rod called a grozing iron. Individual pieces of glass were usually quite small, but when several pieces were joined together using specially cast strips of lead, they could form sections as large as thirty inches square. As each window section was finished, copper rods were attached to the outer face to provide additional rigidity against the wind.

On the scaffolding, window makers installed iron bars between the mullions and tracery to support the weight of the glass panels and to hold them in place. Although single pieces of glass were usually no larger than eight inches square, the finished windows could easily reach heights of forty feet or more.

In November, as in every previous winter, the stone-work was covered with straw and dung to prevent frost from cracking the mortar before it had completely dried. While many of the masons went home during the coldest months, those apprentices who couldn't afford the time off worked in the quarries. Stonecutters and sculptors took up residence either in workshops or in smaller sheds between the buttresses of the choir, which were a little easier to heat. They continued shaping stones and tracery or carving capitals and statues in preparation for the return of the masons in the spring.

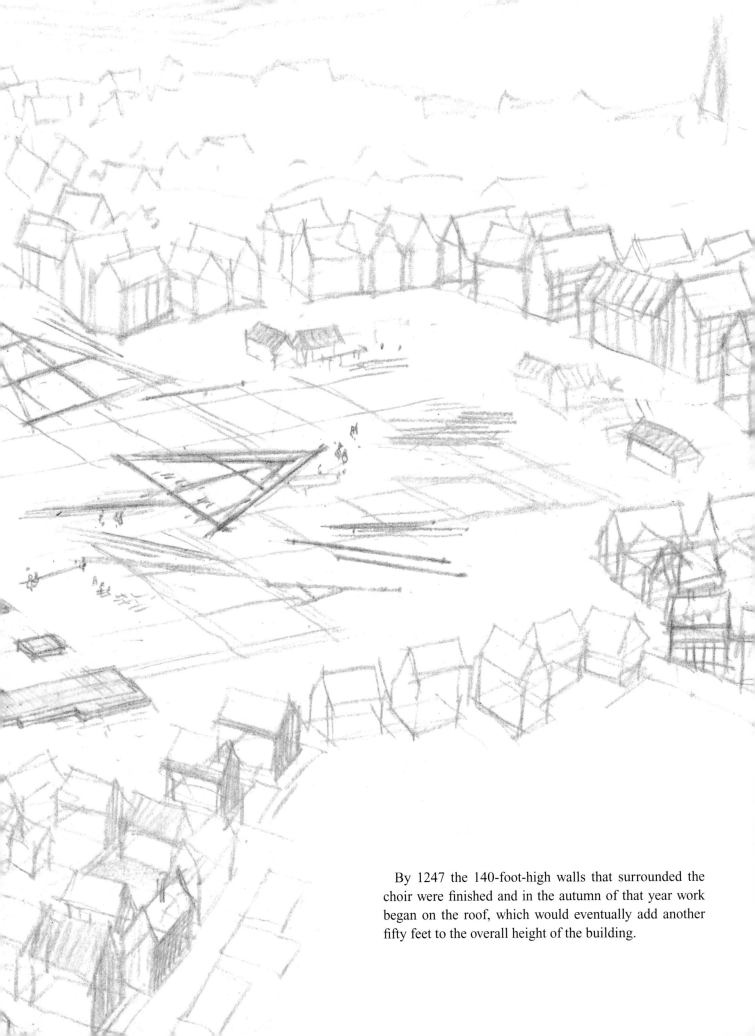

By 1247 the 140-foot-high walls that surrounded the choir were finished and in the autumn of that year work began on the roof, which would eventually add another fifty feet to the overall height of the building.

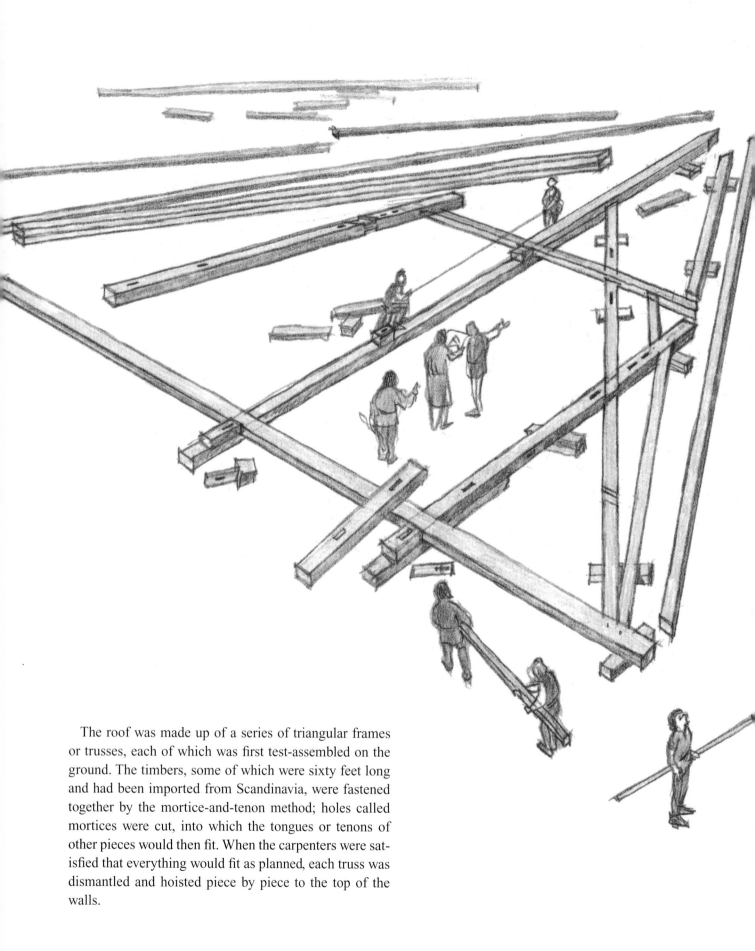

The roof was made up of a series of triangular frames or trusses, each of which was first test-assembled on the ground. The timbers, some of which were sixty feet long and had been imported from Scandinavia, were fastened together by the mortice-and-tenon method; holes called mortices were cut, into which the tongues or tenons of other pieces would then fit. When the carpenters were satisfied that everything would fit as planned, each truss was dismantled and hoisted piece by piece to the top of the walls.

Once the crossbeams were in place, a windlass was set on top of them to hoist the rest of the timber and help in setting up the trusses. As the various pieces were maneuvered into their final position, each mortice and tenon was locked together with oak pegs. When the completed trusses were fastened together, additional timbers were installed, to which rows of wooden slats were then nailed. Before being covered with sheets of lead, all of the timber was coated with pitch to prevent rotting.

By the spring of 1253 the roof was finished and the choir was ready to receive its vaulting. This stone ceiling would spring from the walls about a hundred feet off the ground and rise to a height of thirty feet. Robert of Cormont, who had replaced the aging William as master builder, supervised the erection of new scaffolding high up above the choir on which masons, mortar makers, and carpenters could safely work.

It was during the construction of the scaffolding that the bishop of Chutreaux died. Work stopped for seven days, and on the fourteenth of July 1253, his body was interred in a new tomb in the old crypt. On the fifteenth of September work was interrupted once again, this time for the installation of Roland of Clermont as the new bishop of Chutreaux.

Two types of machines would be used to lift the stones and concrete to the roof for the construction of the vaults. The first was the windlass, of which there were several already in place, and the second was the great wheel. It was large enough so that one or two men could stand inside. Through its center ran a long axle to which the hoisting rope was fastened. As the men walked forward both the wheel and the axle turned, winding up the rope. The great wheel was capable of lifting very heavy loads, the first of which were the large centerings that would temporarily support the vaulting until it could stand on its own.

keystone

voussoir

rib

One by one the precisely cut voussoirs were placed on the centering and mortared together by the masons. When a number of ribs met at the crown—the highest point of the arch—they were locked in place by the insertion of a keystone. A year later, with the mortar sufficiently hardened, the ceiling itself, called the webbing, could be built. Two teams, each with a mason and a carpenter, worked simultaneously from both sides of a vault. The carpenter first installed narrow wooden frames called lagging on top of the centering and across the space between the ribs. The masons then laid webbing stones on top of the lagging. They used the lightest stone possible to reduce the weight.

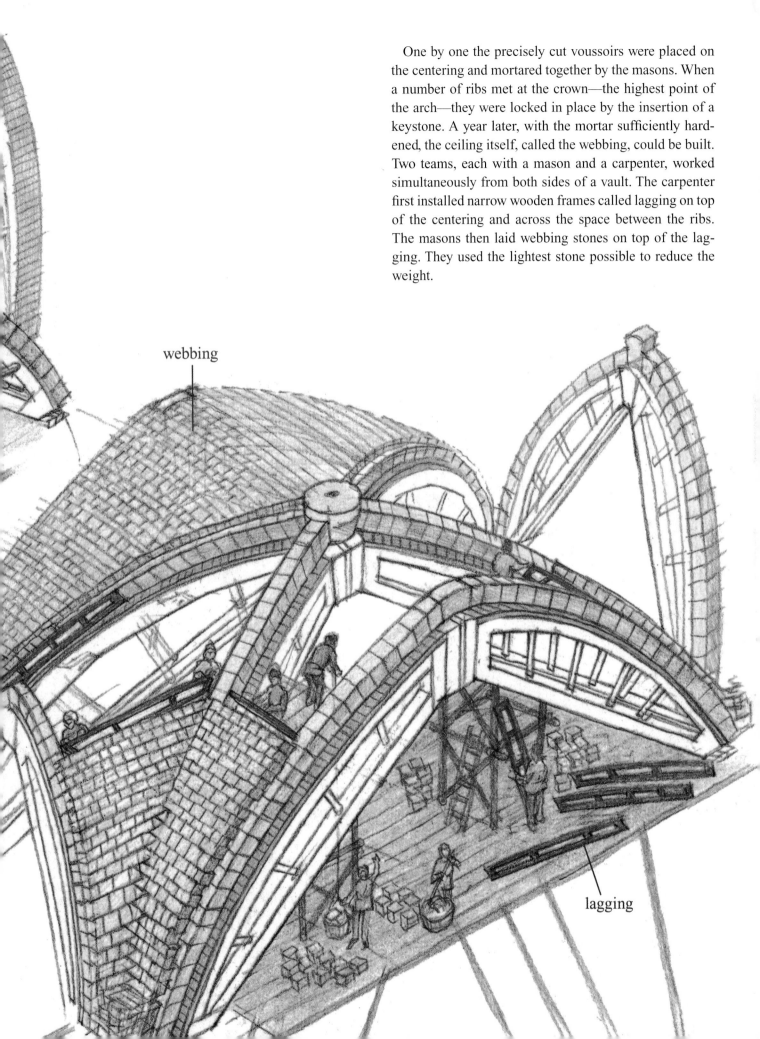

webbing

lagging

Finally a four-inch layer of concrete was poured over the entire vault to prevent any cracking between the stones. The deep cone-shaped spaces left between the ends of each arch and the wall were filled with pieces of webbing and rubble to further strengthen the vault against the outward thrust of the arches.

When the centering and lagging was eventually lowered and moved to the next bay to repeat the entire process, the underside of the webbing was coated with plaster on which lines were carefully painted to give the impression that all the stones were more or less regular. Since no one on the ground would notice the difference, this was primarily done for God's eyes.

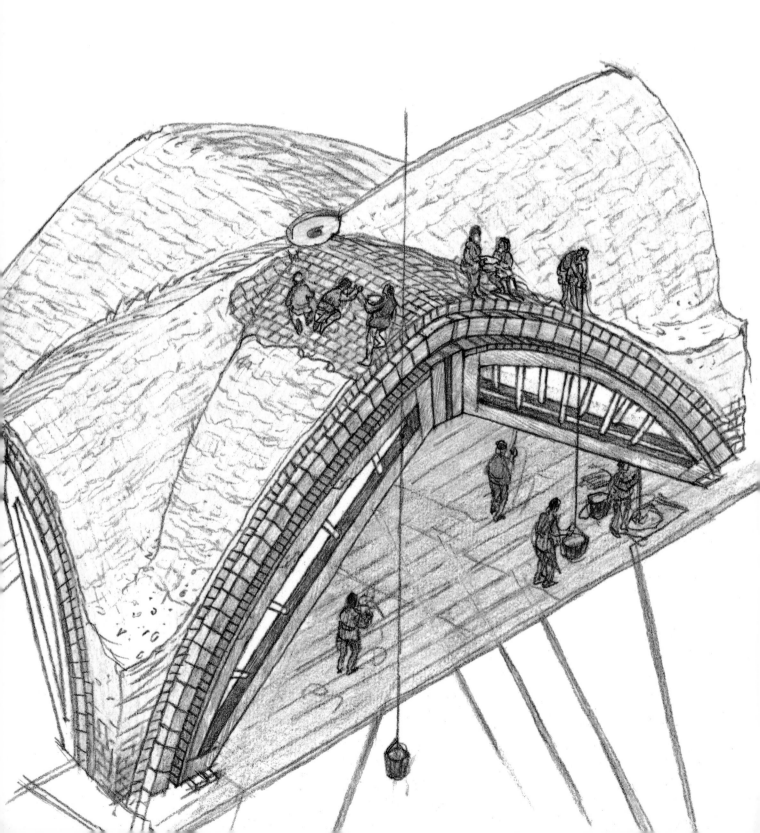

By the time the vaulting was complete, so were all the flying buttresses. The buttresses themselves were capped with steep pinnacles to add extra weight, and various carved stone creatures were set in place to ward off evil spirits. Some of these grotesque creatures also served as downspouts called gargoyles. When it rained, water from the roof would travel across the upper flying buttresses and out through the mouths of the gargoyles onto the ground below.

Once the scaffolding had been removed, the covering over the crypt was dismantled. At the same time, a high temporary wall was built to seal off the choir from the rest of the construction so that it could be safely and immediately used for services.

In June of 1264 during the annual Pentecost celebrations the choir was dedicated with great festivity. But within two years the chapter had run out of money and almost all work on the building was halted. After doubling his own financial commitment to the project, Bishop Roland encouraged the cannons and citizens of Chutreaux to follow his example. And to stir the generosity of those well beyond the city walls, he also decided that various relics from the crypt should be displayed throughout the surrounding countryside for a period of five years.

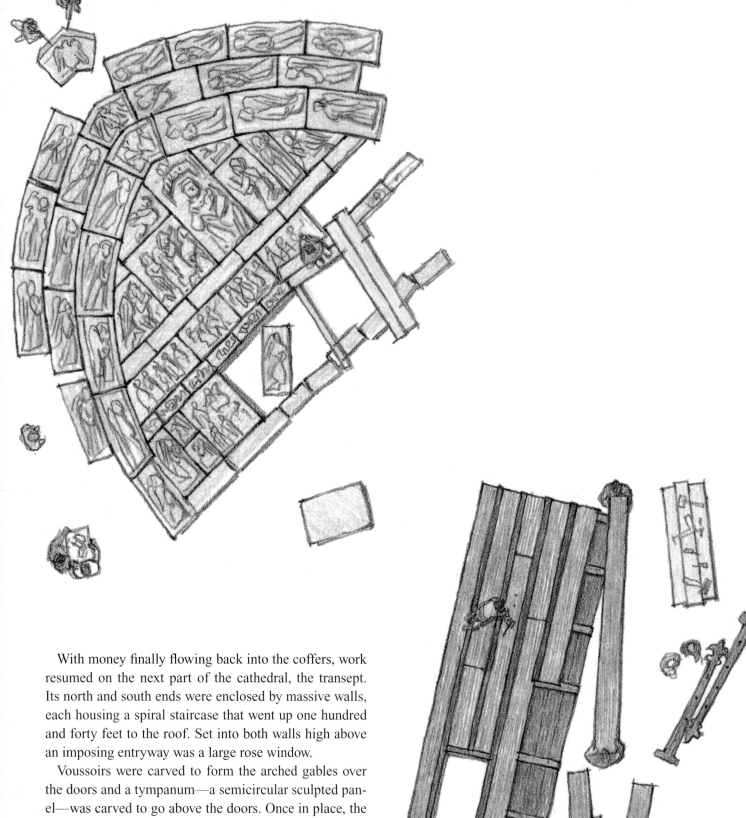

With money finally flowing back into the coffers, work resumed on the next part of the cathedral, the transept. Its north and south ends were enclosed by massive walls, each housing a spiral staircase that went up one hundred and forty feet to the roof. Set into both walls high above an imposing entryway was a large rose window.

Voussoirs were carved to form the arched gables over the doors and a tympanum—a semicircular sculpted panel—was carved to go above the doors. Once in place, the various carvings were painted with vibrant colors. The doors themselves were made of heavy planks joined with cross ribs. One of the blacksmiths had made all the nails for the door and a master metalworker had created the bolts, locks, and hinges.

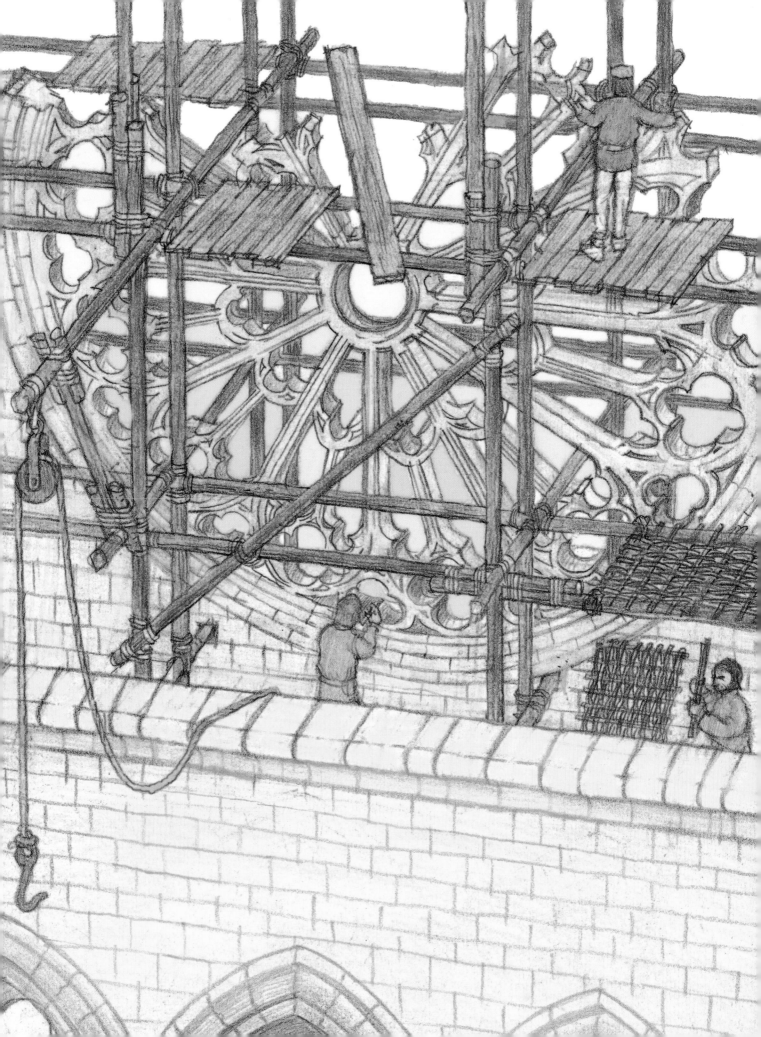

Sixteen years would elapse between the dedication of the choir and that of the transept. After a week of festivities, Master Robert and his workers turned their attention to the piers and buttresses of the nave. At the same time, a group of highly skilled carpenters and roofers a hundred and ninety feet above them began assembling the 150 foot-tall spire. This wood-framed structure was covered with sheets of lead and decorated with sculpture and ornaments.

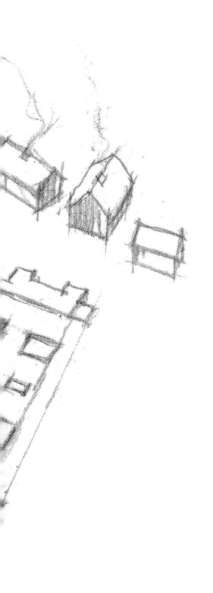

In 1282, as the spire neared completion, Bishop Roland, who had been so eager to preside over its dedication, succumbed to injuries sustained while touring the site.

Out of gratitude for his leadership and great personal generosity, it was decided that he should be buried in the cathedral itself rather than in the crypt. His tomb was built in the aisle adjacent to the choir.

Over the next twenty years construction gradually proceeded westward. By 1302 the centering was in place for the last section of vaulting and within a year the nave itself was finished. As work began on the west front with its two towers and three entrances, the people of Chutreaux dared at last to imagine the completion of their splendid cathedral. But there would be one more small test of their patience and determination.

News arrived from the quarry that the stone now being extracted was no longer of sufficient quality. The remaining building material would have to come from another quarry several miles farther away. As funds were already stretched, the added expense was greeted with understandable dismay. Since fewer craftsmen could now be afforded, the pace of work slowed considerably.

But it never stopped, and for another twelve years the façade climbed slowly but steadily skyward.

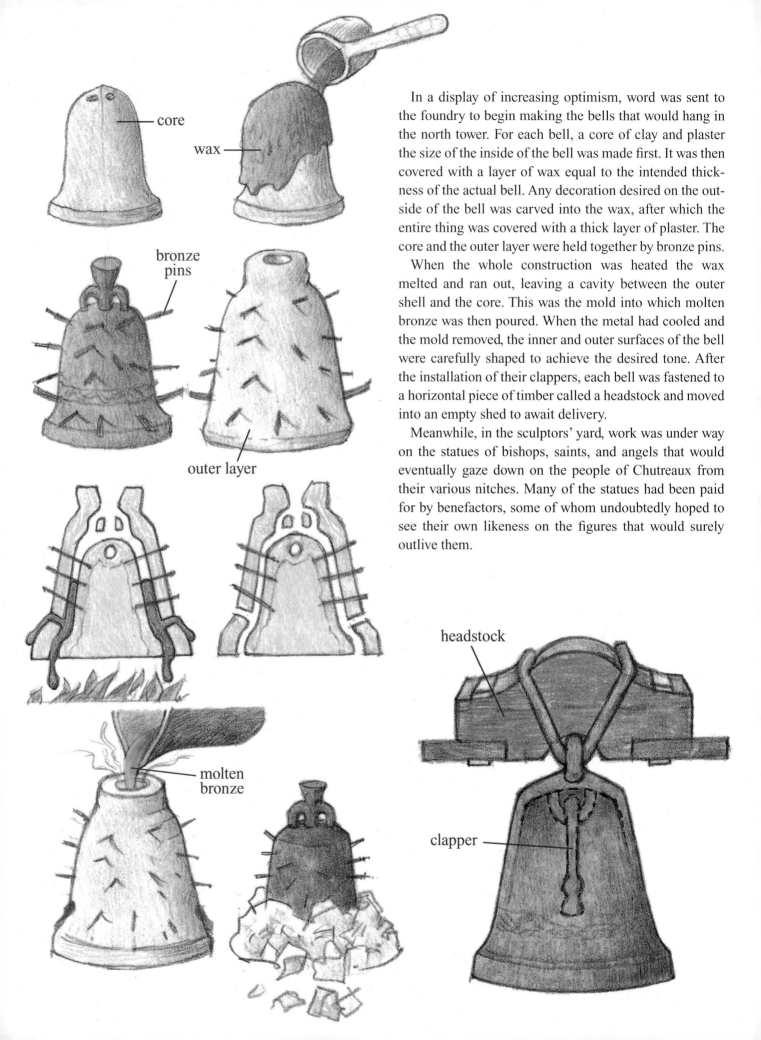

core

wax

bronze
pins

outer layer

molten
bronze

headstock

clapper

In a display of increasing optimism, word was sent to the foundry to begin making the bells that would hang in the north tower. For each bell, a core of clay and plaster the size of the inside of the bell was made first. It was then covered with a layer of wax equal to the intended thickness of the actual bell. Any decoration desired on the outside of the bell was carved into the wax, after which the entire thing was covered with a thick layer of plaster. The core and the outer layer were held together by bronze pins.

When the whole construction was heated the wax melted and ran out, leaving a cavity between the outer shell and the core. This was the mold into which molten bronze was then poured. When the metal had cooled and the mold removed, the inner and outer surfaces of the bell were carefully shaped to achieve the desired tone. After the installation of their clappers, each bell was fastened to a horizontal piece of timber called a headstock and moved into an empty shed to await delivery.

Meanwhile, in the sculptors' yard, work was under way on the statues of bishops, saints, and angels that would eventually gaze down on the people of Chutreaux from their various nitches. Many of the statues had been paid for by benefactors, some of whom undoubtedly hoped to see their own likeness on the figures that would surely outlive them.

The bells were eventually hung from a sturdy timber framework called a bell frame. Both were protected from the elements by a wooden roof and shutters. A wheel attached to each headstock was connected to a long piece of rope. When a bell ringer below pulled on the rope, the bell rocked back and forth, forcing the clapper to strike the wall. The ringing could be heard for miles.

By midsummer 1314, the cathedral was complete, and on August 19 the bishop and the chapter led a great procession through the narrow streets, returning with the entire population of the city.

Inside the cathedral, colored light streamed through the windows while candles flickered beneath the arches of the triforium. As the choir began to sing, the building filled with beautiful sounds and everyone there, most of them grandchildren and great-grandchildren of the men who had laid the foundations, was filled with tremendous awe and great joy.

For ninety years the people of Chutreaux had shared a single dream, and at last it had been realized.

GLOSSARY

AISLE The part of a church that runs parallel to the main areas—nave, choir, and transept—and is separated from them by an arcade.

APSE The semi-circular or polygonal end of a church, usually the east end.

ARCADE The row of piers and arches that separate the main spaces of the cathedral from the aisles.

BUTTRESS A large stone pier built against or connected to a wall to provide extra strength.

CAPITAL The form, usually of stone, that supplies the visual transition between the top of a column and whatever the column supports.

CATHEDRAL A church of any size that contains the cathedra, or bishop's chair.

CENTERING The temporary timber framework that supports the stones of an arch until the mortar between them has set.

CHOIR The section of the church east of the transept that is sometimes raised above the level of the nave. It is called the choir because traditionally this is where the choir stands to sing during the service.

CLERESTORY The topmost part of the church building, the windows of which illuminate the central portion of the interior space.

CROWN The highest part of the arch, where the keystone is located.

CRYPT A lower level of a cathedral, usually below ground, that is used for burial or as a chapel.

FLYING BUTTRESS In a cathedral, a stone arch that carries the outward forces of the vault to the buttress.

HURDLE A movable work platform made of woven twigs.

KEYSTONE The central locking stone at the top of an arch.

LAGGING Temporary wooden frames used in the contruction of vaulting.

MORTICE AND TENON A method of fastening one piece of wood to another. A mortice, or hole, is cut into one piece of wood while a tenon, or projection, the same size as the hole is whittled out of the other piece. The tenon is then tapped into the mortice and the two are locked together with an oak peg.

MULLION The narrow upright stone pier used to divide the panels of glass in a window.

NAVE The central area of a church where the congregation usually stands.

PIER The pillar or column that supports an arch.

RIB The stone arch that supports and strengthens the vault of a cathedral.

TEMPLATE The full-size wooden patter used by the stonecutter when he has to cut many pieces of stone the same size and shape.

TRACERY The decorative carved stonework of a medieval church window.

TRANSEPT In a Latin cross plan as at Chutreaux, the section that crosses the nave, usually separating the nave and the choir.

TRIFORIUM The arcaded story between the nave arcade and the clerestory.

TRUSS A triangular wooden frame. The roof frame is constructed of a series of trusses fastened together.

TYMPANUM The sculptural area enclosed by the arch above the doors of a cathedral.

VAULT The form of construction, usually of brick or stone, that is based on the shape of the arch. Used for the most part as a ceiling or roof.

VOUSSOIRS Blocks of stone cut in wedge shapes to form an arch.

WINDLASS A machine for hoisting or hauling. In the Middle Ages this consisted of a horizontal wooden barrel with a long rope fastened to it. The barrel was supported at both ends. When it was turned the rope would gradually be wound up around it.